TESLA'S WALK

TESLA'S WALK

AN INVITATION TO TESLA'S COLORADO SPRINGS

JIMMY SENA

atmosphere press

Published by Atmosphere Press

Cover design by Felipe Betim

Atmospherepress.com

CONTENTS

To my three little sparks:
Isabelle, Abigail, and Arielle

PREFACE

Thank you, friends, for picking up this book and making your way to this page. If you are browsing in one of my favorite local bookstores, even better, and I envy you. Places made of words—bookstores and libraries, even a friend's bookshelf—are mysterious and wonderful places to inhabit. I find bliss and solace surrounded by words despite not knowing which of them I need. Books know, though.

Now, a disclaimer: if you were hoping for a book chock-full of equations and charts with timelines and patent numbers, I will try to let you down easy. This, friends, is not one of those books. There exist already scores of brilliant biographies and technical papers devoted to Nikola Tesla, some of which you will see listed in the back of this book and which I am so grateful to have read in my own research. Instead, what I hope you find between these covers is equal parts story, poetry, travel narrative, and living, local history.

2024 marks the 125th anniversary of Nikola Tesla's visit to Colorado Springs. He remained here for almost eight months: May 17, 1899–January 7, 1900. He accomplished with experiments and electrical manipulation some of his most important work. He brought along intellectual triumphs and emotional baggage from his youth and early career struggles. He left quietly, owing money to individuals and to the city itself, on his way back to New York. These subjects I invite you to explore in those many excellent biographies.

This book takes a different path, a walking path, with space on every page to meander in and out of thought and imagination along with Tesla. I wanted to explore the humanity of this creative, complicated, and scientific man in our town, my hometown, on the same streets, even in a few of the same buildings that still stand today. The storytelling format attempts to emulate this walking

1

and this humanity, flowing from thought to thought and stanza to stanza during one autumn day in 1899. It begins as he wakes in his room at the Alta Vista Hotel and culminates that evening in one of the calamitous electrical events which he unintentionally inflicted on the El Paso Electric Company.

All names of persons and places, every location and street, and every unique description (do you hear me, strange sprinkler railcar?), is factual and found among primary source materials including newspaper articles, interviews, period photographs, period maps, and the perpetual founts of wisdom known as the *Colorado Springs City Directories of 1898 & 1900*. One can tell a thousand stories just by reading through these directories (I am totally serious). What I found delightful was their habit of listing the occupation of an individual which then allowed me to make surprising and fun connections. As you wander through these poems you will see quotes from Tesla appear here and there, reminding us of his powerful command over language. Above all, Tesla's own *Colorado Springs Notes, 1899–1900*, have been an irreplaceable source for reasons both obvious and truly unexpected. I invite you to peruse them; they are enlightening and mystical.

You will find a map in the back with Tesla's walk laid out, along with some useful (or not) tidbits of history. To help envision what Tesla saw 125 years ago, images of colorized postcards from the era are scattered throughout along with clarion black and white period images from Colorado College's *Century Chest* photograph collection (further information about all the images can be found in the explanatory notes). As well, I've included some words describing what Tesla would see now along the same path as it inevitably becomes your own to follow and alter as time progresses. Each time you walk the path it changes a bit as you notice something different, sit in a new spot to examine a building, gaze down the length of a street from a new perspective, ponder the sky, or refresh the eyes on Pikes Peak. My path has certainly evolved over the course of writing the book, and it still does, never failing to bring joy.

Tesla was a complex and layered genius. He was both mentally gifted and mentally challenged. He possessed eccentricities well known then and better understood now. It is safe to say he suffered from social anxiety and compulsive disorders in varying degrees: his obsession with the number three, his ever-growing fear of germs, his need to turn right after leaving a building, his need to count steps in various languages (he spoke eight), just to name a few. He lost his mother a few years before arriving in Colorado Springs, and he was closer to her than anyone else, before and after her death. His childhood in Smiljan seemed nurturing and idyllic but tragic as well. This dichotomy followed him, persisting in the belief that genius may very well be a blessing and a curse. His enduring legacy, however, is singular: magnificent.

I hope to see and meet you on our downtown streets during the cooling autumn months, perhaps with a warm beverage in hand, walking the same path, imagining Colorado Springs 125 years ago. I invite you to use this book as a travel guide of sorts, allowing the verse to interpret our downtown in a different kind of way, and when you explore the additional material after the story, perhaps you will see the pictures through another lens and read the history with another eye.

And please make time for the clouds. Tesla loved our clouds.

MORNING AT THE ALTA VISTA HOTEL

~

Alta Vista Hotel, Colorado Springs, Colo.

Bells.

Nikola? Nikola... the bells.

Bells.

Nikola? Wake up boy.

Bells.

I hear you Mama, yes... I... hear...

Morning sunlight meddles in the dreaming.
Church bells meddle in the ear.

He lifts his eyes. Heavy, again.
Dreams of his *majka* emerging more often
since autumn arrived,
sprouting fresh and green in the heart
as leaves outside lose their own green
in the turning harvest.

The bells in his dream,
he still hears them clearly.
They toll from Smiljan,
from the Church of St. Peter and St. Paul,
just beside his childhood home
where his *otac* served the town's congregation.

The warm, sweet sound of its two bells,
foggy in his half-dreaming mind.

A tintinnabulation of memory still blooming.
Overtones woven with the golden thread
of his mother's voice.

Tesla rises and walks to the window.

The bell which woke him,
its song now landing softly over his dream.
Sound lowered by a weightless breeze.

He draws aside thin curtains from his small
second-story hotel window, gazing west,
not on his beloved boyhood church
but on St. Mary's Catholic Church
and its delicate octagonal bell tower.

Its red-orange brick is striking in the morning light,
and close,
perhaps a hundred feet away.
His elevated position endeavors a unique view.

St. Mary's on Kiowa Street offers its loud bell
to the entire community.

A sturdy 1897 Buckeye Foundry Bell,
swinging and banging and rolling.
Piercing the air, perforating his dream
with its temporal sharp edge.

These two churches, their bells,
and one dream collects them all.

The top of St. Mary's tower just outside
his hotel window is built of eight open arches.
Window frames,
each with their own perspective of the foothills.
A rope wheel is visible beside the bell,
rocking with it, the sight scarcely ahead of the tone.

Further west, morning sunlight
paints the mountains with abundant,
saturated sheets of yellow and white,
pulling green tree and purple earth
and rusty rock closer.

A single pine.
How is it possible to see a single pine tree
thirty miles away?
Yet, it is.
This mountain air is so clean and clear and pure.

And the light.
How much candle-power is thrown at these mountains?
Trillions upon trillions upon trillions
of candles, surely.

Every green needle collects its spoils
with millions of other needles carpeting these branches
on millions of trees carpeting these mountains.

Tesla's gaze is drawn up, following the contours,
the rising and falling of layered hilltops
resting upon one another in ways inevitable.

A small, single cloud lingers above a low hill.
A shadow below twists it with invisible silk.

Tesla turns from the view,
his mind clearing and settling now.

He surveys the small hotel room
for things out of place, as is his habit.
Three hats hanging on wall posts,
three pairs of shoes underneath.
He checks the window lock three times.

Time to wash and dress.
The experimental station beckons.

Now in his vest and tie,
his dark, pressed trousers and waistcoat,
his hat.

I come here for work,
reminding himself.

There are great laws I wish to discover,
principles to command.

Miracles to witness.

Tesla steps into the hall, closes his door,
checks the latch three times.

_____

Room 207
The Alta Vista Hotel
West side of Cascade Avenue
between Kiowa and Bijou Streets
Colorado Springs
1899

At times it has seemed to me as though I myself heard a whispering voice, and I have searched eagerly among my dusty bulbs and bottles. I fear my imagination has deceived me, but there they are still, my dusty bulbs, and I am still listening hopefully.

—March 11, 1896

Tesla walks the length of the carpeted hallway
to the now familiar spiral staircase
winding itself down and around
an ornamental bronze elevator shaft to the first floor.

The polished bronze plate halfway down reads
Smith-Hill Elevator Co., Quincy, Illinois.
Tesla has ridden manual Smith-Hill elevators in
Pittsburgh while consulting for Mr. Westinghouse,
but not an electric model like this.

The cage is lovely but far too claustrophobic.
Wrapping a mile of copper wire around it
would most certainly make it a respectable
oscillator, however. He smiles to himself.

I notice you contemplating the elevator cage again,
Mr. Tesla. Have you finally decided to take it up?

A.J. Albert, Head Clerk at the Alta Vista,
greets Tesla often and with genuine excitement
hoping to engage him in conversation.
He enjoys Tesla's foreign accent seasoned
with an educated and modulated tone.
Sounds within sounds.
The curiosities of language.

Not today, Mr. Albert.
I admire the bronze work very much, though.

Tesla remains in place
looking through the bronze cage
and the new angles created
by a simple turn of the head,
this way and that.

Will you be taking your breakfast downstairs today,
sir? I am happy to arrange a table in the west dining
room, the views are brilliant this morning.
I lingered on them earlier while walking down Tejon,
particularly crisp and clear indeed.
It is our nature to take for granted the beauty
in this place but all we need do is look up.

Tesla finally turns and walks towards
the middle of the lobby.
His black shoes are in crisp contrast
to the light ash floors.

You remain as clear-sighted as the mountain view,
Mr. Albert. Yes, thank you, please arrange
a breakfast plate—
the chive omelet if you please, and potatoes,
perhaps an orange.
I will take it at one of the writing desks
as I have notes to organize.

Mr. Albert nods and heads toward the kitchen
posthaste.

Spinning on his heels, Tesla begins to the south side
of the lobby toward the writing desks,
passing reading chairs filled with patrons
holding the *Evening Telegraph*, last night's edition.

He more often than not takes breakfast in his room
to avoid side glances and passing comments
in airy sotto voce.

He naturally shirks the many social calls
made upon him, yet is very approachable
and will answer questions if given the opportunity:

Telephony without wires...
I must study the conditions of the upper strata...
In this high altitude there is much to be learned...
The barn structure is about 18 feet high with a 12-foot roof...

—Colorado Springs Notes, June 4, 1899

When asked after his arrival in town
why he gave out so little information about his work,
he remarked innocently that he had not realized
he made a secret of his work. All one must do is ask.
Since, reporters approach him often for interviews.

The inertia of human opinion persists regardless.

A dark slim foreigner.
I guess we all thought him crazy.
To tell the truth, he was not taken very seriously.

His name may be in these same papers scattering
the parlor. Tesla requires privacy to work but
appreciates public validation of his accomplishments.

Civil, communal discourse propagates
scientific curiosity.

Dramatic headlines conjure magic in the imagination.

HE MANUFACTURES LIGHTNING BOLTS

Nikola Tesla, the Wizard of Electricity
has an Instrument Which Can Kill
30,000 People in an Instant

—Evening Telegraph, August 12, 1899

Tesla walks the ochre and white ash checkerboard floor
wondering how many squares he has stepped upon
since arriving at the Alta Vista four months ago.

His counting of steps has been ruined
by this mesmerizing floor.
Broad beams of morning light from the
east windows pass over the squares
and play tricks on his counting compulsion.

Every morning the light is different.
The angle of sunlight turns,
tuned by the Music of the Spheres.
It plays the floor grid as a cosmic instrument.

Tesla settles at a Cheveret desk,
slides some letter paper from its stack in the drawer
along with a pen and inkwell.

*proposed structure to elevate terminal to a height of
140 feet from the ground...*

*post very strong and reaching nearly
to the roof of the building...*

keep the wood safe against the streamers...

*pipe above the roof will be π x 20 x 12
(6+5+4+3+3+3)...*

copper ball having nearly 30 sq. feet...

*wind pressure will be considerable but it will be
fairly safe...*

      —*Colorado Springs Notes, September 22, 1899*

As Tesla continues to rewrite his notes,
Albert reminds the kitchen staff about
Tesla's needs:

You must approach Mr. Tesla from his left and use
your left hand to place his plate down
and you mustn't crowd him in any way.
How many clean napkins do we have left? ...Only 11?
Right, then. You must present Mr. Tesla
with 9 napkins, flattened and folded,
and wear white gloves, please.
You do recall that Mr. Tesla requires napkins
in quantities of three, yes?
Good, thank you, gents.
Mr. Tesla should be at a writing desk presently.
Please bring him his plate when it is ready
and report to me after such.

Tesla eats his breakfast while he works
as is his habit
and finds a stopping place,
pocketing the orange for the day ahead.

Raising his head, breathing deeply,
his gaze unexpectedly submerges
into the painting on the wall
above the writing desk.

Attached to the picture frame
is a small metal plaque with the words:
Pike's Peak from Manitou Springs, Colorado
Leslie James Skelton, artist

~~~

Tender, reddish-pink wildflowers
near the bottom invite the eyes up the canvas
over prairie grass sharpened by fibrous white,
leading to a grove of dark pine trees,
then to another,
finally to the mountain
etched by two thin currents of white clouds
giving depth and securing the peak's massive place
in the center.
High clouds parted by scant blue sky remain.

~~~

Tesla emerges from the image,
deep in thought and emotion,
a memory cooling his eyes like a breeze.

I propose to send a message
from Pike's Peak to Paris.

His words spoken in this very room to a reporter
upon his arrival in Colorado Springs on May 17th.

Not to happen.

The scientific man does not aim at an immediate result. He does not expect that his advanced ideas will be readily taken up. His work is like that of a planter—for the future. His duty is to lay the foundation of those who are to come and point the way.

—The Problem of Increasing Human Energy, June 1900

Another deep breath to strengthen the resolve.
Tesla stands, as tall as ever, pulling his coat flat
against his trim, angular frame.
He collects his notes and replaces them
into his shoulder bag, his *vade mecum*,
embroidered by his dear mother
which he treasures and repairs
as often as needed.

Turning towards the main entrance he scans
the reading rooms, the writing desks,
the parlor and the office,
the bronze elevator shaft and the spiral staircase,
noting the humanity moving around him,
the electric lights above him,
and the invisible energy surrounding it all.

Albert catches his eye and walks over.

Will you be needing your regular lunch delivered
to your workshop today, sir?
I will confirm it with the kitchen before you leave.

Yes, Mr. Albert, indeed the same. I am grateful.

It is our pleasure, sir. Very well. Shall I ring
for the carriage to take you there now, sir?

No need. I have been requested
for a meeting at The El Paso Club
and will walk there.
After which I will make my way
to the experimental station for the day.
I expect to return rather late as we are culminating
an important sequence of experiments this evening.
The weather today feels especially fitting.

Very well, sir.
We look forward to greeting you tonight
on your return and will have fruit
waiting in your room.

Tesla tips his hat.

Thank you, Mr. Albert.
Adieu.

Tesla leaves the checkerboard floor,
exiting through the main doors of the Alta Vista
onto a spacious stone porch.

He is greeted by several people watching the
goings-on up and down Cascade Avenue,
enjoying the sunny morning and crisp air.

Good morning... yes, it is... how are you...
beautiful day...

Folks are spreading out among
four impressive stone archways,
some leaning on the center stone railing
with its short and stout stone columns.
Two stone staircases lead down to Cascade Avenue.

Tesla inhales slowly,
fills his lungs with clean, sweet Colorado air
and slowly releases his breath.

Tesla walks on the flat dirt of Cascade Avenue
making his way one block north
before turning east on Platte Avenue.

Immediately his eyes spillover with the sight
of the enormous clock tower at
Colorado Springs High School.

The school lies two blocks east of the El Paso Club
on Platte Avenue, Weber Street,
and Cheyenne Avenue.

The latter cuts a diagonal through the block,
leading directly into the walking path
of Acacia Park, catty-cornered from the club.

Tesla is nearly three blocks from the school.
Grand Romanesque architecture
commandeers the sky.

The four-sided tower is capped with a pyramid
adorned by four pointed turrets at its corners.
They emphasize the diameter of four
colossal clock faces showing the time
in each direction.

Tesla spies a small metal ball topping
a flagpole on the school's south side.
A very usable spherical terminal reminiscent of the
copper-coated ball atop the mast at his laboratory
on the plains.

Tesla continues walking east,
crossing Platte Avenue at an efficient angle
and closing the distance to the El Paso Club.

A familiar sight now.
The steep roofs, the ornate gables
and turrets and curved window glass,
the covered front porch,
and more of the reddish brick
in such common use around town.

This social club was once a Victorian residence
and occupies the northwest corner
of Tejon Street and Platte Avenue.
Town leaders and Colorado Governor Charles Thomas
welcomed Tesla here on May 23rd
at a banquet held in his honor.

Today's meeting may very well be similar.
His reluctance to attend another
social event is equaled by his impatience
to get to his lab for work.

Nonetheless, the opportunity to impress
upon the public his reasoning for such
revolutionary scientific experiments
is a necessary skill to practice.
Some of those here today did arrange
for his laboratory to receive free electricity,
after all.

Tesla mounts the curb beside the building
and notices his friend and business associate
Leonard Curtis standing on the porch
in anticipation of his arrival.

Curtis, a past-assistant to Tesla's patent attorney in
New York, moved to Colorado Springs a few years
earlier for his health and suggested the town as a site
for the inventor's wireless telegraphy experiments,
owing to the dry climate and abundance
of lightning strikes.

Afternoon thunderstorms,
Curtis explained, can not only be powerful
but also quite predictable during
the spring and summer months.

The high altitude with its thin, dry air
has proven favorable for electrical transmission
to and from the clouds, and in dramatic fashion.

In his experimental station, Tesla utilizes two sensors
to record lightning strikes at variable distances,
one measuring up to 20 miles and another up to 100.

Observations made last night. They were such as not to be easily forgotten. First of all a magnificent sight was afforded by the extraordinary display of lightning, no less than 10–12 thousand discharges being witnessed inside of two hours. Some of the discharges were of a wonderful brilliancy and showed often 10 or twice as many branches.

–Colorado Springs Notes, July 4, 1899

Tesla climbs the stairs and reaches the porch
of the El Paso Club.
Curtis extends a hand
which Tesla does not reciprocate.

Ah yes, sorry old friend. You will remember, yes,
when you introduce me to the gentlemen inside?

Tesla prefers not to shake hands.
He contracted many infections as a boy,
including cholera,
which makes him very fearful of germs.

Yes, of course, Nikola. We will manage quite fine.
It is good to see you.

Tesla tips his hat.

Likewise, Leonard, I am quite happy to join you all
here today.

Curtis holds the door for Tesla
and the two enter the foyer of the El Paso Club.

Rich wood paneling lines the walls
of this refined entry room while a fireplace
to their left creates a warm ambiance.
A staircase with delicate wooden railings
directly across the room leads up and to the left.

Pardon me gentlemen,
may I present Mr. Nikola Tesla of Serbia
coming to us by way of Budapest,
the Paris Opera House, the Chicago World's Fair,
and if you are to believe him, as a billiards hustler
in New York City.

Polite applause and laughter immediately follow
this oration and several faces, some familiar,
approach Tesla in the foyer.

Tesla keeps his hands clasped behind his straight
back and bows graciously as names are spoken,
introductions given, and acquaintances renewed.

R. C. Miller, the steward of the club,
motions for the group to repair to the adjacent room
as drinks are handed out.

Windows on the east wall and turret windows
on the south fill the room with warm, natural light.
Another fireplace can be seen along the north wall
of this large, carpeted room.

Dr. Edwin Solly takes the initiative.

Mr. Tesla,
thank you for sparing a few minutes of your workday.
We will not keep you too long, I assure you,
and you can soon continue to Knob Hill.
A group of us suggested this casual meeting
while leaving church on Sunday.

Tesla scans the faces surrounding him.

It is indeed my pleasure, Dr. Solly,
and I am grateful to see you again.

Tesla first met Edwin Solly back in May
at the welcome banquet here.

Solly, a past president of The El Paso Club,
is known as a leading citizen constantly moving about
the social and public enterprises of the town.
He is a respected medical doctor
known for his research of combating tuberculosis
in this dry climate, indeed,
the very reason he moved here from England.

Solly's organized social soirées
grew into a Café Society which rivaled those
of any large city and helped lead
to Colorado Springs' adopted moniker, *Little London*.

The room fills with low voices in conversation for a
few moments as men meander in and out
of Tesla's vicinity.

Mr. Tesla, please allow me to introduce our group.
We are all professors and fellow mathmeticians
from Colorado College.

Florian Cajori, Professor of Physics,
P.E. Doudna, Professor of Mathematics,
and William Strieby, Professor of Chemistry
and Metallurgy.

All smile and thank Tesla for the opportunity
to meet him.

Professor Cajori asks if Tesla's experiments using
the massive induction coil in his laboratory are
proceeding well since pausing work on wireless
telegraphy, as he read in the *Evening Telegraph*.

Very well, yes, and the completion of the coil
instigated my change of focus.

Professor Strieby mentions with glee
that the other night he noticed
a blue and white glow emanating
from the barn on the plains.

I share your enthusiasm Professor Strieby,
and I am constantly in awe of nature's power
revealing itself in this place.

Professor Doudna asks if the summer grasshoppers
proved bothersome to his experiments.
The infestation of 1898 has already become
legendary.

I found that grasshoppers avoided
the highly charged atmosphere,
but I understand the overabundance
of these creatures last summer was indeed
something to, shall I say, witness?

The four of them laugh and share a fun moment.
Tesla begins to feel a kinship, a rare thing for him.
A sense of community begins to float over the group.

May I add, Professor Doudna, that butterflies
seem not to be afraid of the barn at all.
They appear rather attracted to the area
when we engage the equipment.
They fly in curious patterns around us which we
now refer to as winged halos. It is quite a sight.

Strieby runs a finger around Cajori's head
in good fun, then finds his hand swatted away.
They all laugh and the rest of the room turns toward them.
Cajori muffles his laughter then uses the levity to announce
a celebration scheduled for February.
The 25th Anniversary of Colorado College.

Mr. Tesla, have seen the new Perkins Fine Arts Hall
on our campus? Construction has finally finished.
It is a marvelous space, and I am helping to organize
the celebrations beginning with a private exhibit
featuring many of our local artists.
At the risk of embarrassing Dr. Solly, his portrait
is among the lot, painted by the very talented
Mrs. Anne Parrish.

Cajori continues, nary a breath,
and Tesla fears a recruitment may be in the offing.

Leslie Skelton's canvases will also be featured
alongside paintings by a town favorite, Maude Bemis
...and... (breath)... watercolors of European scenes by
the popular architect Thomas MacLaren are on my
own list of favorites, as are works by a new resident
painter and sculptor, Artus Van Briggle,
and... (breath)... would you have anything to donate or
would you like to attend as our guest of hon...

Tesla bows and interrupts Cajori,
thanking him for this invitation.
Doudna and Strieby take Cajori by the arm
hoping to break him from his revelry.

That solves it, he hopes.

More murmurs of politeness, then Solly speaks up.

Mr. Tesla, if you would permit one more introduction
before departing for your laboratory,
this is R.J. Bolles, president of the
Cheyenne Mountain Country Club at Broadmoor.

Bows and pleasantries.
Bolles, clearly on a mission, immediately invites
Tesla to visit his Club as his special guest for polo,
or golf, or cricket, or general sight-seeing of the
incomparable Cheyenne Mountain at sunset, noting
the Rapid Transit Railway stops at his club on its
way to the Casino at Broadmoor each evening.

I am grateful for your warm invitation, Mr. Bolles,
and will remember to accept when I find it suits the
schedule.

Tesla goes on to say that the majority
of his experiments are accomplished
around and after sunset.
Bolles is nonplussed,
smiling through his teeth in defeat.

Solly senses the awkward scene,
pats Bolles's shoulder with good humor
and changes the subject.
He quickly returns to the anniversary conversation
and mentions Grace Episcopal Church, where he is
junior warden, is also celebrating
its 25th anniversary.

I walk past your church on Pike's Peak Avenue
nearly every night, Dr. Solly.
I enjoy its modest design...
it reminds me of my childhood church.

Solly observes in empathetic silence,
waiting for clarity to return to Tesla's face.

That is remarkable. How so?

Tesla's mind is usurped by time and emotion.
A quick intake of breath, but this is stopped,
and nothing said.

A memory unfolds,
a hidden memory,
sudden even to him,
and elegant.

He remembers his majke standing outside
their church, waving,
while he watches from a window.

Such a remote and distant time, and yet,
fresh waves of memory seem mountainous.
The mind like a fragile boat slicing up and down
breezy drifts and sunken waves,
pulled and pushed,
at times the horizon disappearing all together.

I... perhaps another time, Dr. Solly...

Tesla refolds the memory,
attaching a golden hue this time,
hoping to find it again.

Conversation through the room has finally lulled
and Tesla hands his glass to the steward.

He brushes his hands on his coat,
his capacity for cordialness exhausted.

Alas, gentlemen, I bid you all adieu
and thank you so very much for your hospitality.
My assistant will have already arrived at the
laboratory setting up for the day's experimental
ledger. We have a busy day ahead.

Tesla bows to the group, raising a hand in retreat.

He slides from the room into the foyer,
an elegant move which one can see
has served him well in crowded scenarios.

Curtis attempts to catch him,
the sounds of thank you in his wake.

Tesla is already outside,
the door closing behind him.

Our virtues and our failings are inseparable,
like force and matter.
When they separate, man is no more.

−June 1900

THE WALK DOWN TEJON STREET

~

North Tejon Street, Colorado Springs, Colo.

On the stone porch of the El Paso Club
Tesla grasps the corners of his waistcoat,
pulling down and flattening the fabric,
stretching the buttonholes,
feeling his shoulders angle down,
asking these memories to run down as snowmelt.

While descending the stairs he notices patterns
in the red brickwork on the porch railing
and tiny, tessellated brick cubes
decorating the length of the railing then up, up,
up the side of the rounded turrets
along the eastern expanse of the building
until the bricks turn the corner
and he can see them no more.

Tesla turns south surveying the length
of Tejon Street, active with townspeople
and a railway car. A horse whinny echoes.

Walking across Platte Avenue at an angle
he reaches the northwest corner of Acacia Park.
In the Alta Vista lobby he has heard the words
Acacia Place... North Park... High Park...
all referring to this same block of land.
Puzzling.

It is at first inviting then mesmerizing
looking into Acacia Park from this corner.
The rows of trees seem indeterminate.
They reach, they pull,
they fool the eye without moving an inch.

The park is crisscrossed with broad, diagonal
walking paths of mounded dirt, lined with
20-foot-high trees planted a dozen feet apart.
The trunks are tall enough for branches
to clear the view of a hundred other trees
preparing to meet at the center.

At this moment the sun is overhead,
casting shadows of leaves onto more leaves
in a recursive trick of the light.

Leaves on leaves,
on shadows,
dark on dark.

The ground underneath brightening again
at the uncovered park center,
then darkening and brightening yet again.

In the park center lives a painted iron water fountain
topped by a decorated finial, open on every side.
Sunlight is piercing down through the breach
without a leafy bastille to block its yellow gilding.
The painted black iron gleams like a beacon.

Tesla enters the park and follows a path,
noticing people of all manner
eating lunches on benches lining the paths.
Children are tossing and hopping over stones.
Birds are sounding as they do the world over
during a warm midday.

The noise of one's footsteps in a park is unique.
It is integral to the living moment.
Tesla remains present,
finding peace in the nature of his footfalls.

Sound is the shadow of movement
through time and space.
Never repeating, never ceasing.

Arriving at the crossing,
Tesla sees a little girl at the water fountain
attempting to drink.
Her hat is repeatedly slipping down over her face
as she giggles to herself with each sip.
She finishes with a forearm wipe,
reaching up in a tall stretch
to touch the arching metal black cat
topping the decorated iron finial.

A memory opens up in the moment
and Tesla is back home with his beloved
family pet, his black cat, *Macak*,
with whom he spent day after day,
playing and rolling around outside,
lying in cozy corners inside.

Luminous memories emerge
of petting *Macak* at night.
Static electricity leaps from his back
in the dry winter air of Smiljan.
What a gift to see you here, old friend.

Tesla, allowing a diminutive smile, turns to the right
and follows the walking path leading back to Tejon.

Ambient noise gradually gathers around his head
as he nears the southwest corner of the park.

The intersection of Tejon and Bijou
remains popular throughout the day.
The more one walks down Tejon
toward the downtown business block,
the busier, as sidewalks begin to lose
their hold on pedestrians.

Tesla begins to see red fire alarm boxes
pepper the street poles.
He spies the tower of St. Mary's
popping up directly west.
He crosses Bijou and is suddenly amid
two and three-story buildings.

The disjointedness of the park
with this neighboring block is striking
and a testimony to the usefulness
of a public park for this community.

Standing on the southeast corner
of Tejon and Bijou enlivened by
a spiritedness no longer latent,
Tesla is consumed
by a confluence of senses.

Sight. He looks west along Bijou Street,
up and over the small rise a few blocks away,
then, at last, to Pike's Peak.

The potent midday sun is drenching the mountain,
pouring down and over
every massive and minuscule thing
without a cloud to contrast the blue firmament.

Smell. The empyrean, irresistible smell
of fresh-baked bread from the Auberer Bakery
just across the street.
Lunch lines form as tributaries from their source.

Sound. The echoing, inharmonious blast
of a train whistle
from the Denver & Rio Grande Depot
down and over just a few blocks.
Tesla disembarked at this station upon his arrival
then was taken by horse up the hill to the Alta Vista.

Beginning to walk south on Tejon now,
Tesla passes the Perkins Crockery Co.
beside the bakery across the street,
recognizing the name from the dishware
at the Alta Vista.

Dishes, he has learned, are strangely in demand.
Tesla has overheard Albert discussing
weekly crockery orders with a gentleman
from Ivywild calling himself Mr. F. Perkins,
a nervous and jubilant businessman
who sways back and forth while delivering
brown paper-wrapped stacks of dishes,
gambling with fragility at each breath.

He can theorize the connection.

The Antlers Hotel on Cascade Avenue,
the first, the largest, and the most prestigious of all
Colorado Springs' hotels, burned down last October.

The Alamo Hotel and Tesla's own Alta Vista
have been shouldering the extra business,
even to the point of adding rooms and services.

The Alta Vista's basement barbershop
has been inundated since the Antlers' shop closed,
the line leading to the basement entrance consistently
extending up to street level.
Kitchenware supplies seeming immune to such issues
have instead proven to be among the ancillary
wayfarers of the hotel shortage.

Tesla catches a glint from a sign posted
on the building to his left, shoulder high,
Odd Fellows' Hall, Third Floor,
a popular public meeting hall for society gatherings
and clubs, and a location to which he has been invited
by his assistants who work
at his experimental station.

Continuing on and approaching Kiowa Street,
to his left he spots some brushed top hats
in the window of Giddings Bros. Department Store.

When last here Tesla purchased three roles of felt
for insulation against heat transfer in the main.
These hats look inviting, though.
Perhaps a new one for All Saint's Day.

Across Kiowa, the sight of a hulking building
encourages him to cross Tejon to avoid the crowd.

A sign on the brick proclaims
The J. J. Hagerman Building
in bold stamping.

Hagerman Hall on the Colorado College campus
with its lovely Roman arch comes to mind.
These buildings could not be more different.

Crossing Tejon Street in a serpentine manner
to avoid carriages and townspeople,
Tesla himself becomes as electrical vibrations
in random movement.

As like the earth itself...
conducting and transmitting energy.

As like the upper air strata itself...
perfecting a conducting path.

These are the chaotic and brilliant hypotheses
which bring him here to Colorado Springs.

He makes it to the west side of Tejon
narrowly avoiding a dog lunging at a fluttering bird,
sliding to a stop in the dusty gutter against the curb.

As I see life on this planet, there is no individuality. It may sound ridiculous to say so, but I believe each person is but a wave passing through space, ever-changing from minute to minute as it travels along, finally, some day, just becoming dissolved.

—Electrical Experimenter, 1919

Stepping up onto the curb, collecting himself,
pulling down his waistcoat,
Tesla walks a few feet down the block
to stop under the small awning
of the Opera House.
The front doors are ajar, and he wanders in.

A hallway leads his feet
towards the back half of the building.
Event postings chronicle the walls.
Light-colored, vertical wood paneling
welcomes the view into the lobby.
Two staircases mirror each other on either side.
The doors of the theater are propped open.
Tesla continues and peeks in,
feeling his weight lifted immediately
by the cavernous space.

The opulent decoration and sculpture above
the proscenium arch grabs the eye first.
A wreath of leaves surround
a portrait resembling Shakespeare
while the typical masks
of Comedy and Tragedy
hang on either side.

Directly below hang several layers
of luxurious curtains in rich burgundy and gold
along with slender green and gold pennants
hanging every few feet.

The main curtain is pulled open to either side
of the stage revealing bright, grand living quarters
full of chairs and lounges,
golden bowls and chalices,
Mediterranean tapestries and oriental rugs.

A screen upstage of painted Roman arches and
columns completes the set with a flat authenticity.

The mind needs only the tiniest grain of life
to resurrect a memory.
A sound, a smell, a touch.

In this case, a light.

The chandelier in the center
of the theater is refined and graceful,
hanging under a sandy-yellow dome
encircled by dark, intricate woodwork
blending with paint and extending onto the ceiling.
Concentric circles of dangling crystals
orbit the arm of the chandelier along the base
fashioning a pellucid silhouette.
The luminaire is unlit but the hanging crystals
are refracting nonetheless,
drawing light from invisible sources,
scattering it to the dome above
if only to be drawn in again as Ambrosia.

Tesla is brought back almost twenty years
to his days working for Edison
at the Ivry-sur-Seine Lamp Factory in Paris,
designing and installing the first
lighting systems in the Paris Opera House.

The astonishing chandelier hanging
in the rarified air of the Palais Garnier
is a glowing heart of Parisian aesthetic expression.
It is just as elegant in its incredible scope,
just as refined in its immense candle-power,
just as triumphant in its 1,900-seat theater
as any chandelier he has seen before or since.

Tesla feels incredible memories of working
in that building among his French colleagues.

While guiding power line through
one of the immaculate Carrier-Belleuse
torchères statues at the foot of the Grand Staircase,
a Parisian friend enticed him with a tale:

Under the Opera House lies a series of tunnels,
even an underground lake,
where prisoners of the French Army
were kept by the Paris Commune
before the army retook the city.
Occasionally a body surfaces from under
the Palais Garnier and floats up to the Seine.

Tesla dwells in this waking dreamscape.

His focus eventually returns
to this smaller but no less elegant chandelier
hanging under its gentle dome.

He turns now,
gliding silently out of the darkened theater,
nodding to a passing gentleman while
moving past some posters on the hallway wall
and reading the lineup.

A series of Shakespeare productions:

The Merchant of Venice
Hamlet
The Tempest

A Traveling Hypnotist.

A program for John Phillip Sousa's band concert
a few months ago.

A framed playbill of Oscar Wilde's
International Tour from 1884.

Emerging from the Opera House onto the sidewalk,
Tesla turns right and immediately hears Mr. Albert
from the Alta Vista speaking to another man
in front of a bookstore display window.

Mr. Tesla, what a pleasant surprise.
I apologize, my manners.
Allow me to introduce Mr. Low.
Historian, scholar, and proprietor
of the very fine Low's Book Store.
We were discussing the addition of a reading library
in the hotel near the writing desks.
Would you have any suggestions for a book selection?
The hotel will be happy to create a shelf
of your favorites.

Tesla tips his hat.

Indeed a pleasure, Mr. Low.
Thank you, Mr. Albert, I am happy
to recommend some authors.

Low mentions that he has read about Tesla
in the papers for years and is pleased
to finally make his acquaintance.
Albert and Low continue to speak
but the sounds soften and blur into susurration.
A distance grows between them as Tesla sees
a set of books by Mark Twain in the window.

Twain and Tesla.
Here is an unlikely but genuine friendship
brought to life through the powers
of literature and science in equal measure.

Tesla remembers fondly being given Twain's books
while suffering yet another serious illness
during his youth.

He credits Twain's stories with helping him
to recover completely, and when the two met
at the New York Players' Club 25 years later,
Tesla told him so, bringing Twain to tears.

As the two became friends,
Tesla enjoyed very much hosting Twain
in his New York laboratory,
asking him to partake in experiments
showing that electrical current moving
through one's body can illuminate light bulbs
held in the hand.
Electrified X-rays permeating these same hands
revealed the inner workings of bone and muscle.

Tesla recognizes some of the titles of course,
intending to mention these very books
to Albert and Low for the reading room.

His focus, soft with remembering,
stirs up his own reflection in the glass,
barbed and restless.

Tesla turns south, walking away without a word.

Albert and Low glance at each other,
wondering in silent unison.

Albert offers that Tesla often appears preoccupied,
a busy man with busy ideas.
He must be off to his laboratory on Knob Hill.

Low, an expert in Medieval literature,
quotes Sir Thomas Mallory:

It is well seen by you,
for since ye have departed from your mother
ye would never see her,
ye found such fellowship at the Round Table.

They watch Tesla along Tejon.

Or perhaps, Mr. Albert,
we watch Merlin,
afoot to Pendle Hill.

Twain and Tesla, Spring 1894

There is no one who does not speculate about the questions of his existence, asking whence he comes, whither he is going and what in reality he is.

—May 1899, during a stop in Chicago
on the way to Colorado Springs

THE WALK ALONG PIKE'S PEAK AVENUE

~

Bank Building, Northwest Corner of Tejon Street & Pikes Peak Avenue

Tesla makes his way to the northwest corner
of Tejon Street and Pike's Peak Avenue,
pausing for a breath,
craning his neck up to the sun,
closing his eyes,
feeling the warmth.

The sounds of falling water draw his attention
to the right.

An odd Studebaker Electric Car Sprinkler
is throwing sheets of water onto the dirt.
It is rolling along the rails
where streetcars typically amble.
A curious, mechanical abdomen with wet wings.

The sprinkler car slithers toward the end of the block
where Pike's Peak ends at Cascade
and slowly veers left along the rails, making its way
another block south to Huerfano Street.

As the strange, aqueous sight clears,
Tesla focuses on the second Antlers Hotel
emerging piece by piece from the ashes of the first.

Workers walk and climb and hang from scaffolding.
One can look into, through, and out
window-sized holes in the unfinished outer walls,
empty spaces inside lit by sunshine,
darkened by shadow, dusty and lifeless.

A series of stone arches appear half-built
above entryways while two impressive,
fractional towers reach up in a crude way
to some unknown height.

A covered horse-drawn buggy approaching Cascade
begins to turn right and stops.
Passengers no doubt are looking
at the immense enterprise underway.

Two men in suits and hats walk their bicycles
across Cascade from the hotel curb.
Their steps jerk through knobby clumps of dirt
left by carriage tracks.

These six blocks of Pike's Peak Avenue
between Cascade Avenue and El Paso Street
make up the widest street in town.
From here, Tesla notices two sets of
streetcar rails coalescing into one,
drawing his eye to the east toward Nevada Avenue.
This abrupt, wide view pushes away the zany sight
from the other side of the block.

Rows of empty carriages and covered buggies
line both sides of the broad street,
several horses still attached.

Tall, wooden transmission poles
planted along sidewalks
frame the incredible height of this scene.

Trees alive and green mingle with the cut and dead.
They weave their branches among the power lines
strung from cross-arms and insulators.

More power lines span the street at peculiar angles
connecting pole to pole and building to building.
Some are being used by the railcars,
some could very well connect to nowhere
in this lofty chaos.

Tesla looks up through hanging wires
to the cloudless sky as he walks.
Irregular shapes continually shift
from triangle to rectangle to pentagon to octagon
and on to infinity.

Our senses enable us to perceive only a minute portion of the outside world.

—January 7, 1905

Mining offices and railroad ticket windows
alternate up and down the sidewalks.
One can decipher without much effort
that this stretch of Pike's Peak is where most
of the city's business operations occur.

Indeed, it was on the morning of July 31, 1871
when a group of city founders
pounded a stake in the dirt
at the spot which would become the southeast corner
of Pike's Peak and Cascade Avenues.
The heart of Colorado Springs
began to beat right here.

Walking south across Pike's Peak,
Tesla lands on the curb
next to the Mining Exchange.
At the El Paso Club, R.J. Bolles mentioned
that he was also president here.

Tesla observes well-dressed men inside
huddling around wooden boards
with letters and symbols spelling out
mining companies and stock prices.

Tall wooden ladders are rolling around the room,
creating a restive, circus scene.

Tesla begins to walk east on Pike's Peak,
passing a confectionary with fruit for sale
on a sidewalk cart.
An adjoined store, Briscoe Bros. Books,
has a table outside as well.

Oscar Wilde titles catch his eye.
Wilde is still enjoying popularity since his lecture
at the Opera House fifteen years ago
despite the small audience.

Poetry by Yeats.

Several issues of *Blackwood's Magazine*
with a sign advertising
Joseph Conrad's *Heart of Darkness*
as a three-month serial.

A decorated board with the words
If you liked this, try this
is mounted above a copy of Henrik Ibsen's play
A Doll's House,
nestled next to new copies of
The Awakening by Kate Chopin,
and a small sign,
*A St. Louis Woman Who Has Turned Fame
Into Literature.*

A boy on a bicycle skids to a stop
in a dusty cloud against the curb.

His dark gray newsboy cap fails its grip
and topples into the dusty gutter.
That's a lally-cooler, hep it is
the boy yips as he grabs his cap
and whacks it on his legs,
then leans his bicycle against the building
and saunters in.

The *Evening Telegraph* keeps its
newspaper offices here.
The words *C.S. Sprague, Editor*
are etched on a sign above the two front doors.
Tesla walks past the entrance,
feeling a sense of momentum
from the undercurrent of people entering and exiting.
The newsboy hardly creates a ripple in the stream.

Tesla makes it past the Telegraph doors
only to be plunged into a crush of people
in front of the Post Office.

So many citizens are waiting for mail delivery
in lines wrapping around the corner,
elongating further down Nevada Avenue.

He skirts to the left and off the curb
immediately crossing Nevada Avenue,
avoiding two boys on little donkeys
swinging thin tree branches at one another.

Arriving on the southeast corner of the intersection,
Tesla looks back to gauge the line at the post office.
Perhaps a hundred people are waiting
among parked carriages and horses.
A yellow and white parasol poking up like a daisy
shines a meek opalescence over the mass
of brown coats and hats.

Tesla turns east
leaving this sizzle of humanity behind.

The concentration of trees is beginning to thin.

Dwellings and their fences are lower in height now.

Tesla can hear the distant murmur of
Shooks Run Creek.

To his left,
an impressive wooden trestle bridge
spans a considerable gap in the landscape.
Tall trees at the north end grow strong from the creek.

The Atchison, Topeka, and Santa Fe Railway tracks
benefit from the bridge and lead south
to the depot two blocks ahead.

He passes Dr. Solly's church on the right,
Grace Episcopal.
Pairs of narrow stained-glass windows
are set back in the stone,
throwing more light with each passing step.

The rounded altar room on the east side
and its charming, decorative buttresses
comes into view.

The windows on either side
are as tall and slender as medieval balistraria
with arrows at the ready.

The cadence quickens.

Stillness pools within, spaciousness surrounds.

Tesla takes a quieter, deeper look past the city limits.

The sun, leaning now on the western half of the sky
conjures shadows leading a foot or two ahead of each step.

The sky is a peerless, remarkable blue.

Yellow and brown grassy waves
rise and fall on the sloping hills,
seeming more yellow and more brown
against the constant blue.
As close to touching as if floating miles above.

He continues along Pike's Peak Avenue
until its wide, six-block section comes to an end
at El Paso Street.

Here, Tesla is greeted by three bridges.

The walking path continues to the right,
descending a small ravine and over a foot bridge
of planks and nails.
It is flanked by a wooden fence on the right
and a metal one on the left,
the latter for a wider horse and carriage bridge.
Left of that, elevated railcar tracks continue
to a small trestle bridge,
all of these extending over Shooks Run Creek.

Not a soul is near and the songs of moving water
color the whole world.

Echoes bounce from every surface.
Under feet, overhead,
swirling and welcoming.

The dip in elevation to the creek then up again
throws a switch in the mind.

A transition from town to laboratory.

A conversion in the current.

Rising out of the ravine brings a soaring quality
to the landscape, step after step.

Tall wooden power poles carrying his electricity
grow taller with every inch uphill.

A tall, brick smokestack on the campus
of the Colorado School for the Deaf and the Blind
is a campanile on the prairie,
gathering the land, beckoning to those in need.

The campus is atop a modest hill,
beyond which Tesla can begin to see
his experimental station atop a higher hill,
less than a half-mile further on.

A rail streetcar passes Tesla
on its way to Knob Hill Station
where the main line ends
at Institute Street.

The gentle, obdurate duty of its task,
to and fro, there and back,
is destined and admirable.

It is a solitary journey.
It is a path laid out.

Rails attest to forward movement without waste.
The thin metal arm is reaching up,
sliding against the overhead catenary,
gathering electric fuel in a beautiful smoothness.

It is a mesmerizing vision.
It is validation and testament.

The car shrinks into the distance.

Originality thrives in seclusion free of outside influences beating upon us to cripple the creative mind. Be alone, that is the secret of invention; be alone, that is when ideas are born.

−April 8, 1934

~

Tesla walks up the remainder of the hill
following the line of transmission poles,
passing the school on his left.

The oval driveway to the main building
is quite splendid as it wraps around
beautiful green lawns
on its way to the main house.

Insect noises zip at a distance.

Small birds overhead glide in place
against the breeze.

Prairie grasses grow longer here
without feet to flatten them.

Tall, rigorous green stems of purple clover
clump together in patches and lunge
at angles informed by the
equally rigorous prairie winds.
Their gentle upward curves reflect sunlight
in a purple and yellow ballet.

Prairie sky switchgrass is strong and upright here.
Hints of its golden autumn breath
shimmer in the afternoon light.
Blades ride the cuffs of his pants and snap back.
Longer pieces tap the back of his waistcoat.
The same greeting as yesterday's,
but hundreds of different pieces now,
all a bit longer and eager to dance.

Tesla angles left towards the experimental station,
beginning to count his steps in Serbian.

From this distance
the southwest corner of the barn is sharp
and the roof appears already in its retracted state.
The larger of two wooden towers reaches 80 feet
above the loam.
The mast is not yet fully risen.

The angled timbers supporting the barn
from the ground are holding fast.

Walking... three hundred steps counted...

Vertical planks become discernible now.

Wind speed is increasing
with the slight rise of elevation.

Two eight-paneled glass windows
on either side of the central doors
shine a mild glare from the western sun.
Shades cover only the top halves.

Walking... four hundred and twenty steps counted...

A narrow wooden ladder comes into focus,
a scant off-center.

It climbs from the lower roof to the upper
and continues along the high roof
to the base of the tower.

Lattice supports inside the towers
appear to mingle and intertwine.

Walking... five hundred and ten steps counted...

Tesla can now see his assistant Kolman Czito
moving slowly past the open doors,
looking up to the ceiling and around
the massive oscillator and primary coil.

A sign above the doorway at last becomes legible.

Lasciate ogne speranza, voi ch'intrate.

Abandon all hope, ye who enter here.

–*Inferno*, Canto III, Dante Alighieri (1265–1321)

Tesla mounts the wooden platform
and walks into the barn,
relieved to be out of the potent Colorado sun.

Of his two primary dwellings in town,
he considers this is his first,
spending hours too voluminous to count.
Time moves differently here.

Internal walls built of horizontal planks
reach twenty feet high and fifty feet long.

Vertical boards act as ribs,
joining timbers inside the angled wooden roof
rising a further twelve feet
begetting a chapel acoustic.

The smell of dry wood is perpetual incense.

Tesla greets Czito in Hungarian.

Good afternoon, Kol.
I apologize for arriving later than planned.
The meeting arranged for late morning
extended into the afternoon.
I walked here to clear my mind.

Czito nods and waves it off, smiling,
dismissing the formality of it all.

You are a good friend, Kol.

Czito turns to face Tesla.

Thank you Nikola, jószívű vagy.
You are very good-hearted.

Czito then snaps a few times with both hands
breaking the sentimentality.

He returns to one of the extra coils
arranged in the empty space inside
the massive 50-foot oscillator.

Nikola, I have been tuning every coil
to help maximize resonance
for the experiment tonight.
The secondary coil has been problematic again,
but this arrangement should still maintain
the most sympathetic rise.
The streamers tonight will reach new lengths!
Gyerünk!

Czito raises both arms in a giddy gesture.

Fine work, Kol.
I will verify the increased voltage
from the Westinghouse transformer.
We will be manipulating the highest yet
during our work tonight, easily millions of volts.

The pair work well together
in quietness and confidence.
They met in Manhattan when Tesla
was in need of a machinist and mechanic
after parting ways with Edison.

The War of the Currents
might very well have left Edison's grasp
that very moment when Tesla walked out.

Utilizing Tesla's patents,
Westinghouse with his AC power
bettered Edison with his DC power
and secured the contract to illuminate
the 1893 Chicago World's Fair.

Westinghouse and Tesla
formed a fruitful working relationship
which served them well preparing for Chicago.

Tesla designed twelve fantastic
alternating current generators
to electrify the incredible outdoor exhibitions.
Without wires he illuminated phosphorescent lighting
utilizing high-frequency fields.

27 million visitors beheld the magnificence in Electricity Hall,
and the massive three-story AC Switchboard
used to manage power throughout the fairgrounds
became a miraculous destination,
so efficient as to require only one technician.

The Tesla Polyphase System secured
AC power for the future of humanity.

Tesla Polyphase Exhibit at the 1893 Chicago World's Fair

There is something within me that might be illusion as is often the case with young delighted people, but if I would be fortunate to achieve some of my ideals, it would be on the behalf of the whole of humanity. If those hopes would become fulfilled, the most exciting thought would be that it is a deed of a Serb.

—June 1, 1892, Address at the Belgrade Train Station

Tesla retreats to his small office
in the southwest corner of the barn
to work on a few patent applications
as has become his routine before evening experiments begin.

The sun moves lower in the sky
and nearer to the mountains,
shining more directly through the west windows.

This is his cue to go outside and observe
the formation of any clouds and storms
moving over the foothills.

Nature toys with time
in these approaching moments.

Tesla leaves the barn.

He walks around it three times,

slowly,

orbiting the towering sundial as a planet
tethered by hope and knowledge.

Shadows lengthen.

Yellow light loosens
with a tinge of orange.

Prairie surrounds him.

Tesla pauses facing east,
admiring the architecture
of the Union Printers Home
under a mile away, not yet ten years old.

The low sunlight highlights
its intricate towers and center archway
extending up and over the base of the roof.

The building is bookended by two towers,
the south one taller by far.
Three decorative roof turrets on either side
of the center arch give a satisfying symmetry
to the design.

Much further east beyond the blue horizon,
Tesla follows an assemblage
of enormous white clouds
defined by the might of horizontal light.
As white as snow, as tall as Olympus, as solid as stone.
Buoyant, fresh, and alive.

The Experimental Station is not quite equidistant
between the Deaf and Blind School
and the Union Printers Home,
but the abundance of space around them
blurs the distance.

These three remain alone on the eastern prairie.

Tesla walks back around to the west
and faces the mountains.

Although it is a clear afternoon some thin clouds
form and disperse in front of the hills.

Sunlight piercing a cloud creates thin lines
of dark streamers angling to the ground,
demarcating light from shadow in mid-air.
Columns of energy fit for transporting
gods and monsters from land to sky.

Light is in constant motion,
slow enough to paint the inside of the mind.

Brush strokes

begin in one color,

end in another.

As the sun settles lower,
thin ribbons of cloud emerge from nothingness.
Somehow lit from within,
resembling incandescent metal.

The furnace behind the mountain slowly cools
as these metallic clouds sing with light.

Brilliant white then yellow,
then gold of an earthen depth,
then orange and blood-red,
then dull-red and glowing coal.

Luster never wanes.
The last cloud-fire is extinguished
leaving radiant silver to cool to iron.

The iridescent colors are to my judgment incomparably more vivid and intense than in the Alps. Every possible shade of color may be seen the red and white preponderating. The phenomena accompanying the sunrise and sunset are often such that one is at the point of not believing his own eyes.

—Colorado Springs Notes, August 1, 1899

THE TEMPEST

~

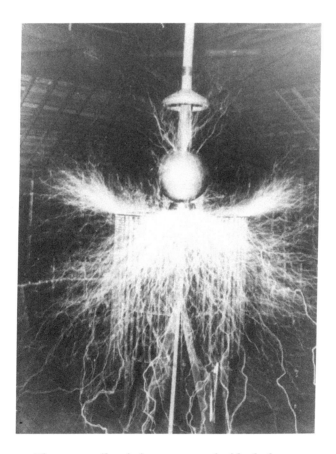

The extra coil emitting streamers inside the barn.

Tesla returns to the barn and he and Czito
raise the mast with its 30-inch copper sphere
through the center of the tower to a height
of 140 feet.

He calls Czito over to the chairs
to once more talk through the sequence of events
for the experiment this evening.

Kol, tonight we will release millions of volts
from the top of the mast.
I will be outside observing the copper sphere
while you manage the switch.
We will first engage the transformer and series
of primary coils.
We will next test the secondary coil by opening it
for just one second to test the charge.
You should hear crackles and snaps.
We may see ambient light.

When I give you the signal,
I want you to close the switch and leave it closed
until I give you the signal to open it.
Please remember to plug your ears with cotton,
and you have your rubber-soled boots, yes?

Czito nods in agreement and pulls cotton
from his vest pocket.
He offers some to Tesla with a wry corner smile
knowing full well he will refuse.

They both smile and stand.

Tesla moves to the office for his coat,
gloves, and hat.

Czito checks his boot laces.

The spread of civilization may be likened to a fire;
First, a feeble spark, next a flickering flame,
then a mighty blaze, ever increasing in speed and power.

—January 16, 1910

Tesla walks outside.
Pike's Peak is now a smooth, deep purple.

The sky above is a smooth, deep blue,
and darker the higher one looks.

Echoes of slim, gray clouds
wisp in and out of existence.

The landscape is flattened now,
attention given to the first few stars
finding their place in this dry, clear boundlessness.

Tesla makes eye contact with Czito and waves.

Czito opens the switch, testing the secondary coil.

Watery, blue light seeps from the barn.

Czito makes eye contact with Tesla, who nods.

Czito closes the switch.

For one second, silence.

Snapping sparks bright blue mist inside the barn cannot see Czito any longer snapping crackling writhing blue snaking up the mast crawling lightning making shadows on the roof snapping popping louder smelling ozone blue mist rolling from the barn sparks in the grass and popping snapping and white-blue lightning slithering up the mast shining the underside of the copper ball and around and swallowing the copper and shooting up CRACK into the blue blackness

and lightning

and lightning

and lightning

And nothing.

And darkness.

And thundering echoes returning

with booming

and popping

and darkness.

The glow retreats, done is the day of toil;
It yonder hastes, new fields of life exploring;
Ah, that no wing can lift me from the soil,
Upon its track to follow, follow soaring!

–*Faust*, Goethe (1749–1832)

Tesla adjusts to the darkness
and makes his way in long strides to the barn.

Czito stands in the wafting, vaporous ozone,
astringent and gloomy.

Kol... why... the switch... why did you open it... why did you stop it?

Czito, coughing, points to the switch, still closed,
and they both notice the lack of power everywhere
in the barn.

All is black.

The phone... test the telephone signal... does the phone... is it working?

Czito hands the phone to Tesla.

Here, yes, here.

Tesla calls the El Paso Electric Company
and erupts into strings of words.

Hello this is Nikola Tesla why have you shut off my power
what have you done to my power?!

A stretched second of stunned silence.

Tesla? Is this your doing?
This is head electrician Frank Jenkins
and I have two primary dynamos burning up.
Have you done this to my power station?
What on earth...
you need to explain what is happening.
We cannot in any way send electricity
beyond the city limits... I need to spray down the...
(huff)... they are ruined.
Ruined.
You are welcome to come here and see the damage.

The call bangs out.

Tesla holds the mouthpiece in silence.

When the great truth accidentally revealed and experimentally confirmed is fully recognized, that this planet, with all its appalling immensity, is to electric currents virtually no more than a small metal ball and that by this fact many possibilities, each baffling imagination and of incalculable consequence, are rendered absolutely sure of accomplishment, humanity will be as ants stirred in an anthill.

—March 5, 1904

Tesla hands the phone back to Czito.
They are both silent.
Czito is still in disarray from the electrical deluge.

Tesla inhales slowly, thinks, exhales, breathes again.

He briefly inspects
the Westinghouse high tension transformer,
the hand crank oscillator,
a few of the metal condensers.
He walks around the primary coil.
He inspects the copper
winding around the large magnifying transmitter.
He smells oil from one of the oscillator switch boxes.

He turns to face Czito
who is wiping his head and face with a rag.

Kol, I believe our night ends here.
Leave the laboratory as you wish.

He walks around the oscillator another time,
slowly,
counting his steps in Hungarian.
Czito counts along silently.

No doubt we will be needing to settle things
with the electric company before continuing anything.

Tesla looks up at a blue cloud
pooling inside the angled rafters.
An invisible breeze leads it out to the dark,
piece by piece,
through the open roof.

Thank you, my friend.

Tesla extends his hand, gloved,
but the gesture is genuine.

Czito shakes it and says goodnight
with a thin smile and grateful eyes.

Leaving the barn in the acrid afterglow
is bracing and burdensome.
The cool air is refreshing
but thoughts of the fire are bleak.

He pauses on the prairie
with a roar of blood in his ears.
He wills his eyebrows to loosen,
his cheeks to lower,
his hands to open.
Night air at last cushions the negative space
between his fingers.

Bell-song arrives from St. Mary's,
unmistakable, over a mile away,
sounding so near as if from the barn itself.
High timbres from Kiowa Street
cleave the dry, dark air.
Tonight it is a familiar poem
found in a strange new book.

Tesla walks slowly,
letting gravity choose his path,
unanchored and without a heading.

He moves south down the hill.
Knuckles of dirt and rock push up through his soles.

He wanders several hundred feet
and stops after the prairie flattens.

Here, gazing through dark
at a ghostly mountain range,
he sits down and removes his hat,
placing it on a tuft of dry, brown grass.

There is a responsibility
that comes with invention, yes.
Nature must remain dominant over the ego.
Yes, of course.
Energy is as fundamental as air.
As fundamental as water.
Everyone who breathes may inhale it.
Everyone who drinks may be nurtured by it.
Every step forward and every fall back
is toward the future, not the past.

Edison's obsession with the illusive
was always futile.
Sound in a box and light in a jar.
They are diffident and forlorn.
Eyes of black pools looking inward without a spark.
Nature will not lose, will never lose,
will break barricades and efface disbelief.

Tesla watches the sky darken even more
as starlight erupts.

Grains of white coalesce in an invisible web,
deeper and brighter with every passing second,
spelling out lessons through time and space.
Through lightning and tempests.

His dreams here of wireless telegraphy
will become reality.
His wishes here of signals riding stationary waves,
the earth becoming a conductor
as sensitive as a tuning fork,
will be studied and confirmed.

Popular opinion may erode futurists
but stars will forever write forgotten words
and ideas yet to be forgotten.

Yet to be believed.

Tesla stands and imagines himself continuing to rise,
leaving the dusty and grassy earth,
his toes the last to lose connection.
He floats over a dark and starlit land
before breaching the top waves of air
and headfirst into the clouds,
taller than ten cathedrals,
stretching to impossible horizons.
Lightning in magical slowness
passes around him from cloud to cloud,
growing inch by inch as if watered by electrons
stacking upon one another.
Under his arms and through his legs
and bouncing off his shoe with a greeting,
What a gift to see you here, old friend.

Still rising, up and out of the clouds now,
higher and higher, finally gazing down
over the roof of the sky.
An electric roof, alive and speaking
with lightning from storm to storm.
Feathery mountains and valleys lit up from within.
Their vaporous inner architecture illuminated.
Cloud beams and wind arches,
sturdy pillars of weightless marble,
and a small house, beside a small church.

~

We are whirling through endless space, with an inconceivable speed, all around everything is spinning, everything is moving, everywhere there is energy. There must be some way of availing ourselves of this energy more directly. Then, with the light obtained from the medium, with the power derived from it, with every form of energy obtained without effort, from the store forever inexhaustible, humanity will advance with giant strides. The mere contemplation of these magnificent possibilities expands our minds, strengthens our hopes and fills our hearts with supreme delight.

—July 18, 1891

AFTERWORD

Tesla ends his night in the middle of what will become Memorial Park. I find this particularly fitting as we follow the path ourselves for one important reason: it is a pocket of open space just as it was when Tesla lived here. We can stop in this moment, spin around, sit and look west, slow down our minds, and contemplate the mountainous sight. Perhaps during our long, luxurious summer nights while bats emerge from their lairs near Prospect Lake. Perhaps during our short, crystallized winter afternoons while Pikes Peak like Odin with his white beard commands the eastern plains. Here is time to be, to connect, to squeeze grass, or snow, or another's hand.

Thank you for reading and for being a part of this walk. It is your walk now, and memories will gather around it quietly.

369 Pike's Peak from Monument Valley Park Colorado Springs

EXPLANATORY NOTES

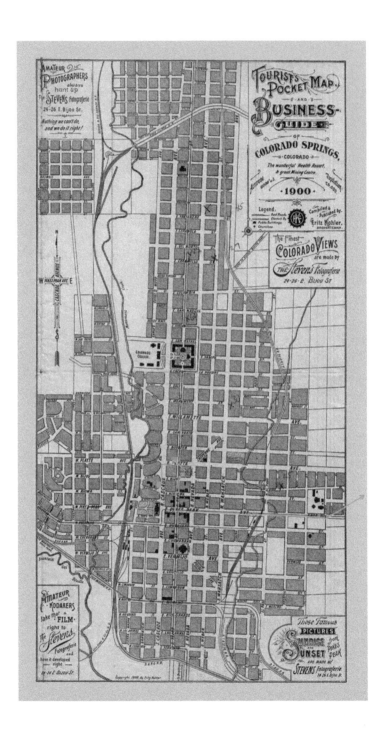

TESLA'S WALK IS LAID OUT IN BLUE.

~

Leave the Alta Vista Hotel.
Walk north to Platte Avenue.
Cross Platte Avenue to visit the El Paso Club.
Cross Platte Avenue to visit Acacia Park.
Walk to the center of Acacia Park.
Walk to Tejon Street.
Cross Bijou Street.
Walk down Tejon Street to Kiowa Street.
Cross Tejon Street.
Walk down Tejon Street to Pikes Peak Avenue.
Cross Pikes Peak Avenue.
Walk along Pikes Peak Avenue to the Colorado School
for the Deaf and the Blind.
Find your way to Kiowa Street between Logan and Foote.
Cross Pikes Peak Avenue to visit Memorial Park.

PIKE'S PEAK OR PIKES PEAK?

Yes, it is common now to omit the apostrophe, but in 1899 this was not always the case. I chose to honor that tradition in the story.

No. 1616 Pike's Peak from Colo. Springs, Colo.

DID TESLA ACTUALLY CAUSE
A CITY-WIDE BLACKOUT?

~

Period sources run amuck around this point, and modern biographies do not agree. In a romantic sense it is quite fun to think it happened! Alas, proof eludes the researcher. We do know that damage occurred multiple times to several power dynamos at the El Paso Electric Company. We also know that Tesla was billed by the El Paso Electric Company for a series of repairs and supplies totaling $245.36 (equivalent to $9,362 in 2024), specifying: *Oct 31 - Time and labor for lineman and helpers putting up new circuit - $79.99*. It is not clear that these events are connected, but one can surmise. Tesla himself, in an August 1917 *Electrical Experimenter* interview, is known to have said: "It was found that the dynamos in a powerhouse six miles away were repeatedly burned out due to the powerful high frequency currents set up in them, and which caused heavy sparks to jump through the windings and destroy the insulation!" The drama was real. The El Paso Electric Company was only two miles away at the most, being situated on the northwest corner of Sahwatch and Cucharras Streets.

PRIMARY SOURCE MATERIALS

~

With the abundance of material available about Tesla I found it refreshing to limit my sources to 1899 newspaper reports and period photographs. Biographies can take you only so far, but pragmatic articles, albeit at times fanciful in the journalistic sense, seem hyper-realistic and riveting. Despite the fact that they have been available for 125 years, I still felt with every article I unearthed that something entirely unknown returned to life. I can't really explain it other than to say it is what every historian feels as giddy motivation. The Pikes Peak Library District and the Colorado Springs Pioneers Museum are primarily responsible, and their value is immeasurable.

The Colorado Springs City Directories of 1898 and 1900 (available through the PPLD), were also of immense help, spawning ideas and offering clarity. Tesla and his laboratory are mentioned on page 365 in the 1900 City Directory with the following entries (note the fun truncation of words here):

Tesla Experimental Station, beyond Deaf & Blind Institute, 1 mi e of PO via Pike's Peak ave.

Tesla Nikola, electrician and inventor, experiment sta e of Deaf & Blind Institute, bds Alta Vista Hotel

Seeing Tesla painted in such a pedestrian manner reinforces the fact that however strange and veiled he seemed, he was still included in the community. Hence is the power of primary sources.

THE 25TH ANNIVERSARY
OF COLORADO COLLEGE

~

This celebration did indeed begin on February 6, 1900 with the opening of an art exhibit highlighting works by local artists in the newly-completed Perkins Fine Arts Hall (sadly gone now, it was razed in the early 1960s).

Science Building, Coburn Library and Perkins Hall, Colorado College, Colorado Springs, Colo.

The three CC professors depicted in the story attended as detailed in a series of newspaper articles describing the guest list and events. Social reports of this nature were very comprehensive. 200 citizens were invited and the newspaper reports are fascinating. Tesla's connection with CC does not end there, as some equipment was acquired by the college after the barn was sold and dismantled in 1904–1905. From the April 27, 1906 edition of the *Colorado College*

Tiger school newspaper: "The electrical engineering department has increased its facilities for testing work by the acquisition of a Tesla high tension, oil-cooled transformer which transforms from 220 up to 60,700 volts, and two high tension oil condensers." As well, this entry from the May 18, 1906 edition of the *Tiger*: "A very valuable addition for the electrical department is being installed this week by Professor Armstrong. The 60,000 volt transformer, used by Nicola Tesla in his experimental station has just been received and will be ready for use within a short time. Professor Armstrong is unceasing in his efforts to build up his department and such work is appreciated by the students and faculty."

Allow me now to offer some historical background about the local artists mentioned in the story and their works exhibited during that week-long event:

Miss Maude Bemis was born into a veritable royal family of Colorado Springs. Maude's sister, Alice, is better known now as a philanthropist and lover of the arts, and these qualities seemed to infuse the entire family. One can find the Bemis name connected to many artistic and academic entities around town.

Mrs. Anne Parish was a portrait painter trained at the Pennsylvania Academy of Fine Arts. With her husband Thomas she had two children: Anne, who became an award-winning novelist and children's book author, and Dillwyn, who studied art in Philadelphia and writing at Harvard. Little Anne and Dillwyn's cousin, Maxfield Parrish, became a revered artist and created a local connection as well. Spencer Penrose, owner of the Broadmoor Hotel, became somewhat of a patron to Maxfield and one day made an unusual request: intentionally paint an inaccurate likeness of the hotel. The next time you find yourself walking around the main Broadmoor hotel, look at the painting behind the registration desks. Here you can see this painting with its two inaccuracies: the lake is placed on the east side of the hotel, and Pikes Peak is directly behind. Penrose believed this incorrect juxtaposition better highlighted the beauty of his property. You can also find several Maxfield Parrish paintings up one level hanging in the mezzanine sunroom adjacent to the lake doors.

Leslie James Skelton was born in Montreal, studied in Paris in the mid-1880s, and moved to Colorado Springs in 1892. Pikes Peak was a subject he returned to again and again. Many of his landscape paintings were reproduced in three-color postcards and sold by the millions. He briefly served as Vice-Principal of the Colorado Springs School of Art and was the President of the Choral Society. Images of the painting which Tesla notices in the Alta Vista can be found with ease; the original was last auctioned off by Christie's in 2011. The Colorado Springs Pioneers Museum has several of his oil paintings and a collection of postcards.

Artus Van Briggle, like Tesla, arrived in Colorado Springs in 1899. At this point in his life Van Briggle likely came from Rookwood Pottery in Cincinnati. Rookwood made history in 1880 as the first large manufacturing enterprise in the country founded and owned by a woman. In a quirky Tesla connection, Rookwood won the Highest Award in Ceramics at the 1893 Chicago World's Fair. Like so many others, Van Briggle came here with hope of relief from the threat of tuberculosis, an ailment to which he eventually succumbed. Van Briggle's name is most commonly associated with extraordinary pottery in Colorado Springs, notably the glazes he implemented and perfected. His work is collected furiously and housed in permanent museum collections worldwide (I am lucky to own a small finger bowl). Like so many other artists, he was trained early as a painter in Europe and some of his work was shown at the Paris Salon. He exhibited nine paintings at the Colorado College anniversary event with subjects from France, Italy, and, naturally, Pikes Peak. One can still walk by his original pottery studio nestled up against the Heritage Garden along Monument Valley Park Trail. General Palmer gifted the land to the pottery and the year 1907 can be seen on the building itself. Colorado Springs architect Nicholaas van der Arend designed a pottery house inspired by his Flemish homeland and in honor of Van Briggle's Dutch ancestry. Hundreds of art tiles and terra cotta mosaics adorn the outside walls of the pottery and the gardens. Colorado College now owns and maintains the building. While you walk around this fascinating bit of local architecture, try to spot the Cat-goyle perched against one of the chimneys.

Thomas MacLaren, like Van Briggle, came to Colorado with the hope of treating tuberculosis. Also like Van Briggle, his painting was overshadowed by another skill. For MacLaren, this was architecture, a vocation for which he will be forever known. His Colorado Springs buildings are well-respected and long-lasting: City Hall, City Auditorium, Ivywild School, the clubhouse at Patty Jewett Golf Course, the Pauline Chapel at Broadmoor, the Manitou Carnegie Library, and so many more. Thomas was born in Scotland, studied throughout Europe, and the 13 paintings he exhibited at the Colorado College anniversary embodied his love for Italian and English churches.

SOME THINGS ALONG THE ROUTE

~

As we linger in Memorial Park, let us indulge a little bit in the places that we passed along the way as we return to the Alta Vista, beginning at Tesla's Experimental Station just up the hill to the north. Look for an alley between Logan and Foote leading up to Kiowa. On the crest of that hill is the most likely location. Tesla found the highest point between the Deaf and Blind School and the Union Printers Home to build his barn, and the topography supports this hypothesis. There have been many ideas posited these past one hundred years regarding the location of Tesla's barn, ranging from the mountain of Pikes Peak itself to the corner of Pikes Peak Avenue and Institute Street where a concrete foundation was discovered in the 1960s. This spot on Kiowa between Foote and Logan, however, is now thought of as the most plausible location. As a kind reminder, please do not loiter or disturb the peace of this neighborhood. The alley acts as garage access to the homes here. Thank you.

It's not surprising that this treasure hunt still fascinates us. Some believe that the land itself may even harbor mysterious electrical forces! Needless to say, the immensity of Tesla's legacy is everlasting and the curious will always find something to follow. The quest is the thing.

In 1904, C.E. Maddocks (aka Charles Maddocks in the City Directory) bought lumber from the barn and told the *Evening Telegraph* he intended to build dwellings in Ivywild. The Ivywild neighborhood lies southwest, nearly three miles from Tesla's barn, and it, too, has a compelling history which we will save for another time. The 1916 Ivywild Elementary School, however, must be mentioned here. It still stands but now operates as a repurposed community marketplace featuring the Bristol Brewing Company, and one or more of the houses surrounding the school may very well be built from Experimental Station lumber. The brewery owners, Mike and Amanda Bristol, recognize this particular recipe for Tesla magic and one can find a Tesla Coil mingling among their giant fermenters in the fermentation hall. They introduced a beer series in 2016 in honor of Tesla, the *Forgotten Genius* series, and their current *World Peace Death Ray* brews grew out of that same series.

Label detail from Bristol's Hazy IPA *(courtesy Bristol Brewery)*

A little background about this proposed death ray: Tesla began teasing the public with his new idea for a particle beam weapon which, by the 1930s, he would name Teleforce. The New York Times conjured a more dramatic description in a December 8, 1915 article: "A machine the possibilities of which test the layman's imagination and promise a parallel of Thor's shooting thunderbolts from the sky to punish those who had angered the gods." Tesla in the same article stated: "It is founded on a principle that means great things in peace." Ultimately, the invention never came to fruition (Or did it? The urban legends are ripe for the plucking). As you play table shuffleboard overlooking the Bristol Brewery fermentation hall, be sure to take in the sight, and dream, as Tesla did, of an invention to put an end to all war.

We can never, truly, be sure of the barn's location, nor the life it lived after its demise. I believe there is no better example than this of the power of local, living history. Let your feet wander and create your own adventure as so many have done before, and we can raise a glass at Ivywild together.

Shooks Run Creek still runs under Pikes Peak Avenue just east of where the road now bends south and becomes Colorado Avenue (which was called Huerfano Street in 1899). El Paso Street no longer connects from the north as it did then. The postcard entitled *Bird's Eye View, Colorado Springs, Colo* just after the title page portrays three bridges over Shooks Run Creek, along with several other notable things: the tower of Colorado Springs High School is in the upper-right quadrant; the Atchison, Topeka, & Santa Fe Railway Station is along the left edge; the second Antlers Hotel is just below the peak.

St. George's Anglican Church now occupies the land where the original <u>Grace Episcopal Church</u> stood, and a few original pieces remain. This building has lived many lives: a church, a Village Inn Restaurant, a nightclub, and again, a church. The current Grace and St. Stephen's Episcopal Church resides on Tejon and Monument.

Grace Episcopal Church, Southwest corner of Pikes Peak Avenue & Weber Street.

If Tesla had followed his same route along Pikes Peak Avenue in August 2020, he would have walked under his own name hanging on the marquee of Kimball's Twin Peak Movie Theater. The film, simply titled *Tesla*, stars Ethan Hawke in the title role and is written and directed by Michael Almereyda. It plays as a period piece but artistic liberties baffle the viewer when they appear (e.g. cell phones). Would he have walked in to see the movie? I think he might have!

(Picture courtesy of Janna Winkle)

177

Post Office Building, Pikes Peak Avenue

Situated near the southwest corner of Pikes Peak and Nevada, the independently owned 1899 Post Office when Tesla visited was at 123-125 Pikes Peak, across Nevada from where the main Post Office is today (first appearing in the 1910 directory). It was conjoined with the *Evening Telegraph* offices and a bookstore. These buildings still stand: the Springs Orleans restaurant operates in the old Post Office and our locally-treasured La Baguette Bakery feeds hungry citizens where the *Evening Telegraph* and bookstore once were. Notice the decorative stone carvings of ribbons and ivy among the second story windows; these are visible in the picture. The newer Mining Exchange building to the east, now a hotel, features a lobby full of interesting bits of history including the old vault door. If you look above its fourth-story windows you can find the building's date. Notice on this building as well the decorative stonework made to compliment the carvings on the original Post office.

Similar to the Post Office, the original <u>Mining and Stock Exchange</u> at 107 E. Pikes Peak and Tejon was situated further west along the avenue in 1899. Tesla, having sold stock himself from his own company, must have recognized the goings-on happening inside.

April 18, 1881, saw the opening of the Colorado Springs <u>Opera House</u> with a production of Alexander Dumas' play, *Camille*. The building's foundation stone came from a Manitou Springs quarry and sandstone adornments were sourced from Cañon City. Period reports glowed: "There are some things in this world that cannot be described by words." The building was hailed as "a perfect gem," and the gallery, "being dubbed with the euphonious name of Garden of the Gods," that phrase already in common use describing the majestic red rocks northwest of town. In 1919 it was converted into a movie theater and in 1947 it was remodeled into a Woolworth store. Today, the Mansion nightclub operates in the old auditorium space, still alive with human creativity.

8528. Acacia Park, Colorado Springs, Colo.

Originally marked as Acacia Place and North Park on early maps, Acacia Park is one of several original downtown parks designed with crisscrossed walking paths, another being Alamo Square five blocks to the south. An important civic building eventually occupied the Alamo block but echoes of its diagonal walking paths remain. I invite you to find them.

January 1893 saw the opening of this iteration of <u>Colorado Springs High School</u> on the corner of Platte and Weber with Cheyenne Avenue cutting a diagonal through the campus. It remained the only high school in town until Wasson High opened in 1959, after which its name changed to William J. Palmer High School in honor of the city's founder. The original 1893 building is lost to history, save for its many impressive pictures and postcard images. The school as it exists today opened in 1940 with additions every few years. The original 1892 school colors of brown and white are still honored today: brown for the mountains and white for the snow.

In 1883 Colorado College Professor and mining engineer James H. Kerr built a Victorian house on the northwest corner of Platte Avenue and Tejon Street as his primary residence. The El Paso Club purchased the building in 1890 and it still functions as arguably the oldest private town club west of Chicago. The original house did not extend as far to the west as it does today. Thomas MacLaren later designed the addition which now stretches west to the alley.

El Paso Club, Northwest corner of Platte Avenue & Tejon Street.

The Alta Vista Hotel was originally built in 1889 and expanded repeatedly in its early years. It was demolished in 1963, leaving one section to survive until 1970. I was very grateful to find an 1899 newspaper article detailing the interior along with actual menus from the dining room. As is the case with many period newspaper articles, the journalist was very conversational and descriptive, even to the point of selling the experience to the reader and leading one directly to the front desk! Images and photos of the Alta Vista were popular choices for postcards and advertising paraphernalia used to proclaim the attractiveness of the city. The Kirkpatrick Bank Building now occupies this lot, and St. Mary's Cathedral with its newer, taller towers and golden spires remains just to the west. Tesla lived the vast majority of his adult life in hotels inside which he required all of his room numbers to be divisible by three. Room 207 is no different.

Alta Vista Hotel between Kiowa & Bijou on Cascade.

Finally, we are back where the day began, on Cascade Avenue. If Tesla, today, were to leave the Alta Vista Hotel and walk north towards Platte Avenue on his way to the El Paso Club, he would pass a parking garage catty-cornered from the hotel and see his name emblazoned with AC power on several Tesla electric vehicle superchargers. I've wondered about this peculiar occurrence for some time. How would he react? He would feel validated, yes, perhaps proud, but also swindled in a sense. Ultimately, I believe he would succumb to science and nature, admitting that his legacy has become extraordinary. A succinct feeling reaching back to his youth, his family, and his earliest days of watching static electricity leap from his cat. To reiterate the 1892 Belgrade quote: *"...If those hopes would become fulfilled, the most exciting thought would be that it is a deed of a Serb."*

N137:-PIKES PEAK FROM PLATTE AVE., COLORADO SPRINGS, COLORADO

ABOUT THE QUOTATIONS

~

Tesla was very articulate and elegant in his speech, and very well read. All quotes come from Tesla save for three:

- Dante, *Inferno*. Another of Tesla's assistants, Fritz Lowenstein, is believed to have posted this warning above the barn doors.

- Mallory, *La morte d'Arthur*. At times I found it difficult not to compare Tesla with Merlin while writing. The same intangible, mystical properties inhabit my mind while I think of them even now.

- Goethe, *Faust*. Tesla was known to have memorized many parts of *Faust*, and he recited them often, including the quote I used in the story. I believe nothing more applicable or profound could have been used after the barn tempest.

ADDITIONAL PICTURES

~

St. Mary's Catholic Church on West Kiowa Street.

High School Building, 1901. Erected 1893.

Locomobile, with view of North Park.

Giddings Block, Northeast corner of Kiowa & Tejon

Hagerman Building, Southeast Corner of Tejon & Kiowa

Northern end of Colorado Springs from Austin's Bluff.

The second Antlers Hotel under construction.

Tejon Street looking north from near Huerfano Street.

The original buildings of the Deaf and Blind School.

Looking west from the main house of the Deaf and Blind School.

A unique perspective of the Union Printers Home before the additions.

Two well-known double exposures of Tesla in the barn.

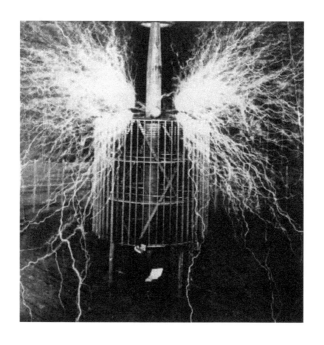

The following images from inside the barn were originally published in
The Century Illustrated Monthly Magazine, 1900 May–Oct.

FIG. 3.   EXPERIMENT TO ILLUSTRATE THE SUPPLYING
OF ELECTRICAL ENERGY THROUGH A SINGLE
WIRE WITHOUT RETURN.

FIG. 5.   PHOTOGRAPHIC VIEW OF COILS RESPONDING TO ELECTRICAL OSCILLATIONS.

FIG. 8. EXPERIMENT TO ILLUSTRATE THE CAPACITY OF THE OSCILLATOR FOR PRODUCING ELECTRICAL EXPLOSIONS OF GREAT POWER.

FIG. 1. BURNING THE NITROGEN OF THE ATMOSPHERE.

ABOUT THE POSTCARDS

~

In researching period photographs a coincidental and quirky bit of history revealed itself: the first colorized, commercially produced postcards were printed for the 1893 Chicago World's Fair (I have yet to find a postcard of Tesla or his Polyphase exhibit but I'm not giving up). These are the types of confluences which secure ideas in a writer's brain. It was a natural choice then to pursue colorized Colorado Springs postcards for the book. The scenes, although at times idealized, were at one time actual photographs, and even seeing these muted colorizations switched my perspective from mere spectator to active witness. All the tools are there for storytelling. They add a cinematic level to the sparse dialogue and a quiet validation that Tesla walked around our streets. I am so lucky to have experienced a different level of our local history through these little bits of cardboard, and equally amazed that some of them still exist! The notes written on them are at times fascinating, at times melancholy, at times illegible. One could send them simply by writing a name and city as a destination. I am thankful that their current destination is by my side.

ABOUT THE PICTURES

~

*"To the citizens of Colorado Springs of the twenty-first century
– to be opened after midnight December 31st AD 2000."*

In 1901 these words were painted on the front of a three-foot, steel-riveted box known as the Century Chest, and 600 citizens gathered in Perkins Fine Arts Hall to watch this Time Capsule be sealed. A century later it was opened on January 1, 2001 at Colorado College, and inside were found over a hundred essays and photographs. The Century Chest collection I explored is that of photographer Frederick P. Stevens whose studio was at 24-26 E. Bijou Street: The Steven's Fotographerie. The images have a remarkable and wondrous clarity. Coincidentally, Frederick's father, H. Hoyt Stevens, was the president and manager of the Alta Vista Hotel when Tesla lived there. A few images are in the story and many more can be seen in the pictures section (you can recognize them from their small captions). They directly reflect what Tesla would have seen in 1899. The Century Chest still resides at Tutt Library, resealed, awaiting the citizens of 2101.

I am indebted to Jessy Randall, Curator and Archivist of Special Collections at Tutt Library, Colorado College, for her help with these incredible photographs.

IMAGE AND PHOTO CREDITS

~

Colorado Springs Century Chest Collection 1901, Ms 0349, Folder 160, Nos. 2, 11, 12, 13, 18, 21, 28, 38, 41, 42, 45, 81, 88, Colorado College Special Collections.

All colorized postcards are from the author's personal collection.

Tesla's Polyphase Alternating Current Exhibit (public domain).

The Century Illustrated Monthly Magazine (v.15 no.2, June 1900) (public domain).

Twain in Tesla's Lab originally published in "Tesla's Oscillator and Other Inventions." *Century Magazine*, April, 1885 (public domain) {{PD-US-record-expired}}.

Experimental Station exterior originally published in Nikola Tesla "The transmission of electric energy without wires." *Scientific American Supplement* Vol. 57, June 4, 1904 (public domain).

Double exposures of Tesla in the barn: Creative Commons/CC BY 4.0 https://creativecommons.org/licenses/by/4.0/

Tourist's Pocket Map and Business Guide of Colorado Springs, Colorado, 1900 (public domain).

Front View of Nikola Tesla's Colorado Springs Experimental Station license courtesy of Tesla Universe.

Panoramic View: Tejon and Platte, and Second Antlers Construction courtesy of the Colorado Springs Pioneers Museum.

SELECTED BIBLIOGRAPHY
AND FURTHER READING

~

Newspaper articles:

"Chronological Table for 1899." *The Evening Telegraph*, Colorado Springs, December 8, 1899

"Tesla in his Work Room." *The Evening Telegraph*, Colorado Springs, June 21, 1899

"Nikola Tesla and his Talk with Other Worlds." *The Evening Telegraph*, Colorado Springs, January 9, 1901

"Tesla's Station is Ready." *The Evening Telegraph*, Colorado Springs, June 2, 1899

"Nikola Tesla will 'Wire' to France: The Wizard of Electricity arrives in City at Noon and will Carry On Extensive Experiments in Connection to Wireless Telegraphy and Upper Atmosphere." *The Evening Telegraph*, Colorado Springs, May 17, 1899

"Nikola Tesla Says he is Not Indebted to Duffner." *The Evening Telegraph*, Colorado Springs, September 6, 1905

"Tesla Developed Wireless Here, Too." *The Evening Telegraph*, Colorado Springs, May 31, 1924

"He Manufactures Lightning Bolts: Nikola Tesla, the Wizard of Electricity has an Instrument Which Can Kill 30,000 People in an Instant – Lightning His Plaything." *The Evening Telegraph*, Colorado Springs, August 12, 1899

"College Anniversary Celebration Begins; Art Exhibition Last Night a Distinct Success." *The Evening Telegraph*, Colorado Springs, February 7, 1900

"Tesla's Electrical Station is Sold for Value of Lumber." *The Evening Telegraph*, Colorado Springs, July 2, 1904

"Banquet given in honor of Nikola Tesla." *The Evening Telegraph*, Colorado Springs, May 27, 1899.

Books:

"Colorado Springs Notes, 1899–1900," Nikola Tesla. Tesla Museum, Beograd, Yugoslavia, 1978.

"Directory of Colorado Springs, 1898." The Out West Printing and Stationary Co. https://ppld.org/sites/default/files/specialcollections/citydirectories/1898CSCityDirectory.pdf

"The Giles City Directory of Colorado Springs, Colorado City, and Manitou, 1900." The Giles Directory Company, 7-8 DeGraff Building, Colorado Springs, Colorado. https://ppld.org/sites/default/files/specialcollections/citydirectories/1900CSCityDirectory.pdf

"Tesla: Inventor of the Modern." Richard Munson. W. W. Norton, 2019.

"My Inventions: The Autobiography of Nikola Tesla." Ben Johnson, editor. Hart Brothers, 1982.

"Nikola Tesla: Experiments and Discoveries." Fall River Press, 2015.

"El Paso Club: A Century in Residence, 1892-1992." El Paso Club Historical Committee, 1992.

ACKNOWLEDGEMENTS

~

Kind and generous contributions from the following people have been indispensable and enlightening and thanking them here does not seem nearly enough. To my editor Colleen Alles: I am so very grateful for your gentle leadership, wisdom, and enthusiasm for this quirky book. Heartfelt thanks to Judy Gudvangen, Susan Paulson, Janna Winkle, and Marianna McJimsey for reading portions of the early drafts and offering corrections, insight, and encouragement in a myriad of ways. Thank you to Fr. David Price of St. Mary's Cathedral for guiding me up, up, up into the bell tower to engage in the tradition of examining the bells, especially the original 1897 Buckeye bell and its hand-welded date which we were able to find inside: 11-19-97 (Fr. Price has recently been named the Associate Director of the Secretariat for Divine Worship and has moved to Washington D.C.). Thank you to Amanda and Mike Bristol for their insight about Bristol Brewery and its fun connection to the Tesla legacy. The staff of the Pikes Peak Library District's Digital Archives are veritable magicians and I could not have accomplished what I have without these archives, not even close, and I thank them a thousand times here. Many thanks to Hillary Mannion, Archivist at the Colorado Springs Pioneers Museum, and to Jessy Randall, Curator and Archivist of Special Collections at Tutt Library, Colorado College, for their time, talent, and generosity. Last but not least, thank you to my 8th Grade English teacher for putting a Jules Verne book in my hands and launching me into a lifelong love of reading.

I frequented several local coffee shops during the extensive research phase of this project when an energetic (and caffeinated) environment was needed: Third Space Coffee, Wayfinder Coffee, Poor Richard's Bookstore & Rico's Café, and The Exchange. This project finally gained speed during the pandemic, and when lockdown was at long last over and our local cafés reopened, only millions of volts could have kept me away from my favorite aromatic and invigorating places.

ABOUT ATMOSPHERE PRESS

Founded in 2015, Atmosphere Press was built on the principles of Honesty, Transparency, Professionalism, Kindness, and Making Your Book Awesome. As an ethical and author-friendly hybrid press, we stay true to that founding mission today.

If you're a reader, enter our giveaway for a free book here:

SCAN TO ENTER
BOOK GIVEAWAY

If you're a writer, submit your manuscript for consideration here:

SCAN TO SUBMIT
MANUSCRIPT

And always feel free to visit Atmosphere Press and our authors online at atmospherepress.com. See you there soon!

ABOUT THE AUTHOR

JIMMY SENA is a Colorado Springs native and a product of School District 11 and the University of Colorado at Colorado Springs. While growing up, riding his bike to the public library to surround himself with books was a constant joy, and this has never changed. His first bookstore job (three cheers for Waldenbooks!) set him off on a lifetime of professional literary adventures and he now makes his living in the university press field. Apart from bookshelves and cycling, he can be found singing professionally around Colorado in classical, choral, and early music ensembles.